Financial Literacy Basics:

How to Manage Debt

Financial Literacy Basics:

How to Manage Debt

2017 Edition

GREY HOUSE PUBLISHING

https://greyhouse.weissratings.com

Grey House Publishing
4919 Route 22, PO Box 56
Amenia, NY 12501-0056
(800) 562-2139

Weiss Ratings
4400 Northcorp Parkway
Palm Beach Gardens, FL 33410
(561) 627-3300

Independent. Unbiased. Accurate. Trusted.

Published by Grey House Publishing, Inc., located at 4919 Route 22, Amenia, NY 12501; telephone 518-789-8700. Grey House Publishing neither guarantees the accuracy of the data contained herein nor assumes any responsibility for errors, omissions or discrepancies. Grey House Publishing accepts no payment for listing; inclusion in the publication of any organization, agency, institution, publication, service or individual does not imply endorsement of the publisher.

2017 Edition
ISBN: 978-1-68217-614-6

Table of Contents

Welcome!

Grey House Publishing and Weiss Ratings are proud to announce its newest series, *Financial Literacy Basics*. Each volume in this series provides readers with easy-to-understand guidance on how to manage their finances. Designed for those who are just starting out and for those who may need help handling their finances, volumes in this series outline, step-by-step, how to make the most of your money, which pitfalls to avoid, and what to watch out for, and give you the necessary tools to make sure you are fully equipped to manage your finances.

Volumes in this series take the guesswork out of financial planning—how to manage a checking account, how to stick to a budget, how to pay back student loans quickly—information necessary to get started on your financial future. Each volume is devoted to a specific topic. Combined, they provide you with a full range of helpful information on how to best manage your money. Individual volumes are:

- Guide to Understanding **Health Insurance** Plans
- How to **Make and Stick to a Budget**
- **How to Manage Debt**
- Starting a **401(k)**
- Tips for Paying Back **Student Loans**
- Understanding **Renters Insurance**
- What to Know About **Auto Insurance**
- What to Know About **Checking Accounts**

Filled with valuable information alongside helpful worksheets and planners, these volumes are designed to point you in the right direction toward a solid financial future, and give you helpful guidance along the way.

Financial Literacy Basics: How to Manage Debt

Sometimes it seems as if everywhere you look, someone wants your money. Maybe you get past-due notices from a credit card company, or warnings about paying your student loan on time. You might be afraid to even look at your mail in case you missed a payment on something last month. If you have bills to pay, you might feel worried about what could happen if you fall behind.

Managing debt can be easier if you understand the meaning of debt and know how to keep it under control. If you have debt, you can make a plan to get rid of it and free yourself from that worry!

What Is Debt?

Debt is money that's owed, and **credit** is money given for use. The person who owes a debt is known as the **debtor** or **borrower**. The person (or company or financial institution) that gives credit is the **creditor**. Examples of debts are money owed on credit cards, car loans, mortgages, and student loans. These are personal debts.

Loans are usually for a certain time, such as several years. The loan agreement includes how many payments the debtor will make, how often, and how much interest will be charged. **Interest** is what the debtor pays to use someone else's money. The debtor pays the interest and the original loan, or **principal**, to the lender. Interest is usually a percentage of the principal. It might be high, especially if the debtor is considered a high risk. This could be because the lender suspects the debtor may have trouble repaying the loan or if the debtor has poor credit.

Credit card debt is a loan, but it has a rolling (open-ended) repayment date. The lender decides how much credit to provide, and the debtor can charge up to the limit. The lender may also increase the limit.

Interest

Each payment you make on a loan includes money toward repayment of the loan as well as interest. In simple terms, if you borrow $100 (the principal) at 10 percent interest and agree to make ten monthly payments, you will pay $11 a month, and the lender will collect $110 by the end of the loan term. You paid the lender $10 in exchange for borrowing $100. The lender charges this interest, known as **simple interest** because it is based only on the principal amount, not only because you are borrowing the money, but also to cover the cost of collecting it, such as paying employees to process payments.

Interest on credit cards is called **compound interest**. Compound interest is interest on the principal amount—but interest is also added to the principal and then interest is charged on this amount. With compound interest, you end up paying much more than the principal.

This type of interest may be compounded, or added, at different intervals. For example, it may be compounded annually, semi-annually, or monthly. The number of intervals depends on the loan agreement. The more often interest is compounded, the more money you will pay.

Collateral

Debt can be **secured**, or backed by something of value. This is called **collateral**. Debt can also

be **unsecured**. A mortgage is backed by the value of the property you are using it to buy, so it is secured debt. Credit card debt is unsecured, because nothing of value is backing it. Secured debt usually involves lower interest rates, because if you fail to make your payments, the creditor can take possession of the collateral.

Good Debt and Bad Debt

Good debt, such as a mortgage or loans for education, can benefit the debtor. Good debt is an investment. It may increase in value or increase your value.

Bad debt is debt used to acquire things that do not create long-term income and lose their value quickly. Debt that carries a high interest rate is also bad debt. The value of debt can be evaluated by looking at its potential to benefit you in the future.

People with college degrees often earn more, so your potential future income could be greater if you take a college loan. These loans also usually have lower interest rates. For these reasons, student loans are usually good debt.

GOOD DEBT vs. BAD DEBT

Good debt is an investment. It may increase in value or increase your value.
- Student Loans
- Mortgages
- Business Loans

Bad debt has higher interest rates or is used to purchase items that lose their value quickly.
- Credit Card Debt
- Car Loans
- Consumer Loans

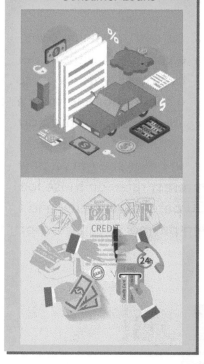

Mortgages used to buy a home are usually considered good debt. They typically have lower interest rates than other kinds of debt and the monthly payments are usually low. Mortgage interest is tax deductible. And the value of a home usually increases over time.

A **home equity loan** is a loan based on the value of your house. For example, if your house is worth $100,000 and you only owe $50,000 on the mortgage, you have $50,000 of equity in the house. A home equity loan uses this equity as collateral. Home equity loans are often good debt, because the interest rates are lower than other kinds of debt. Before getting a home equity loan, however, consider the consequences of failing to make the payments. You could lose the house.

Auto loans may also qualify as good debt. If transportation allows you to earn more, you win. To make the most of the investment, however, the buyer should pay as much as possible at the start, and borrow as little as possible.

Examples of bad debt include credit card debt and cash advance or payday loans. Using a credit card to purchase things you want but can't afford increases your debt but does not provide long-term value. Credit cards usually have higher interest rates.

Payday or cash advance loans also increase your debt without benefiting you. A borrower writes a personal check to the lender and pays a fee for use of the money, but the borrower must pay it back with interest and the fee when he or she gets a paycheck. The interest rates on these loans may be 300 percent annually, and fees for missing payments can be crippling.

How Much Debt Is Too Much?

Even if you have a high income, you might have too much debt to keep up with payments, or you might be paying a great deal in interest. To see if you have too much debt, you can calculate your **debt-to-income (DTI) ratio**. This is a comparison of your monthly debt and earnings. DTI is the percentage of your income before taxes, or gross monthly income, that you use to pay debt.

CALCULATE YOUR DTI

To calculate your DTI, add your monthly payments. This includes mortgage or rent (and insurance and property taxes if you pay them), minimum monthly credit card payments, loans including student and auto, and other debts. Don't count other expenses including gas, groceries, utilities, and taxes.

Divide this debt total by your gross monthly income. This is the amount of money you are paid before taxes are taken out of it. The DTI is the percentage of your gross income needed to cover debt.

Lenders often look at DTI—a lower number means you are less risky. Many finance experts say that DTI should be no greater than 36 percent.

You can calculate your DTI using paper and pencil or use the American Institute of CPA's online calculator at http://www.feedthepig.org/toolbox/calculators/debt-to-income-ratio

For example:

Mortgage	$1,000	+
Auto loan	$280	+
Credit card payments	$220	+
Monthly debt total:	=	$1,500
Monthly gross income:		$3,900

$1,500 divided by $3,900 = 38 percent DTI

If your DTI is too high, you should examine your habits and experiences. Maybe you had to rely on credit cards for a while because you were unemployed. Or maybe you were sick and have large medical bills to pay.

You may have to examine your spending habits, such as restaurant dining and shopping for unnecessary items. You can find free apps to help you keep track of every penny you spend. You can also create a budget to help you see how much you owe and find ways to save. A budget can help you pay down debt.

HOW TO MAKE A BUDGET

The first step is to track all your spending for a month. Write down everything you buy and all the bills you pay. Also keep track of all your monthly income. This may include wages, tips, and any money you regularly get, such as a gift from a relative. If your wages change from month to month, look at paychecks from several months and find the average.

You can find free tools and links to help you manage money at http://www.feedthepig.org/toolbox and http://www.mymoney.gov/tools/Pages/tools.aspx. You can also simply write your budget in a notebook. Take a look at the sample budget on page 6. For more information about managing a budget, you can get further details in another volume in this series, *Financial Literacy Basics: How to Make and Stick to a Budget*.

Divide your expenses into needs and wants. Your needs will include **fixed expenses**, such as rent or a mortgage payment (including property tax), insurance, child care, and loan payments; and **variable expenses**, which change from month to month. Variable expenses include groceries, health expenses, transportation, and necessary clothing. Wants include entertainment, such as restaurant meals and movies, as well as unneeded clothing.

Subtract your monthly expenses from your monthly earnings. If you have money left over, you can save it or use it to pay off debt. If your expenses are greater than your earnings, however, you need to find ways to cut expenses or earn more money to cover them. Start by looking at your wants, and see if you can eliminate spending there. You may be able to reduce needs as well, such as saving on groceries, finding a better rate for utilities or cell phones, or getting rid of a vehicle if you can use public transportation instead. Look at your spending habits. How and when did you spend your money all month? If you bought a coffee or snack every day, you can brew your own at home and buy snacks in bulk to cut costs. Any way you can save money on expenses can help you pay off debt.

BUDGET WORKSHEET

Month/Year: _____

Monthly Income

Wages _____
Tips _____
Other Income _____
TOTAL MONTHLY INCOME _____

Monthly Expenses

HOUSING
Mortgage/Rent _____
Utilities (Electricity/Water) _____
Credit Cards _____
Insurance (Homeowner's, Renters, etc.) _____
Loan Payments _____
Other Housing Expenses (Cable, Internet, etc.) _____

FOOD
Groceries/Household Supplies _____
Restaurant and Other Food _____

TRANSPORTATION
Public Transportation _____
Vehicle Loan _____
Gas for Personal Vehicle _____
Parking, Tolls, etc. _____
Maintenance & Supplies (oil, etc.) _____
Vehicle Insurance _____

HEALTH
Health Insurance _____
Medicine/Prescriptions _____
Other (Dental, Vision, Copays) _____

PERSONAL
Childcare or Support _____
Other Family Support _____
Laundry _____
Clothing, Shoes, etc. _____
Charitable Gifts, Donations, etc. _____
Entertainment (Movies, etc.) _____
Other (Haircuts, etc.) _____

DEBT & FINANCE
Debt (Credit Cards, etc.) _____
Student Loans or Other Debts _____
Fees (Bank, Credit Card, Debit) _____
Prepaid Cards, Phone Cards, etc. _____

MISCELLANEOUS EXPENSES
Supplies (School, etc) _____
Pet Care _____
Other _____
TOTAL MONTHLY EXPENSES _____

TOTAL MONTHLY INCOME _____
- TOTAL MONTHLY EXPENSES _____
= _____

Take Steps to Reduce Debt

Once you have taken stock of how much you earn and spend, look at the interest rates you are paying on debt. Make a list of monthly debts, including student and car loans, credit cards, and mortgage. Continue to pay all your debts, because if you miss payments, you may be charged fees and even higher interest rates. But pay as much as you can on the debt with the highest interest rate. After you pay it off, move on to the debt with the next-highest interest rate and pay that down. Move down the line until you have paid off your debts. You may also want to consider balance transfer offers or debt consolidation.

OTHER DEBT STRATEGIES

Balance Transfers

If you have a credit card that charges a high interest rate, you can find another card with a lower rate and transfer your debt to it. **Balance transfers** allow you to pay off the high-interest amount you owe and pay the lower interest rate on the balance of the loan. This can reduce your compound interest costs as well.

A credit card balance transfer offer typically offers a credit limit, which includes any fees. If you owe $7,000, for example, and your credit limit on the new card is $6,000 (including fees), you will still have to pay the remaining balance. For this reason, focus on transferring the balance from the highest-interest cards to another credit card. A balance transfer can do more than save you money on interest—it can simplify your life by eliminating the need to pay multiple bills. But the balance transfer card's low interest rate may be limited in scope—for example, it may only be for one year. Be sure you know the terms of the balance transfer and consider how much debt you can pay off before the rate increases. The low rate may not apply to new purchases you make on the card, although if your goal is to reduce debt you should avoid making new charges if at all possible.

A balance transfer, once accepted, usually pays the other credit card companies in one to two weeks. Even if you pay off your entire credit card debt using a balance transfer, your account does not automatically close. You must contact the creditor to close the credit card account, and should do so quickly to avoid the temptation to use it again.

Lower Interest Rates

You may be also able to get a lower rate without having to transfer the balance and pay fees. If you are a customer in good standing, call your credit card companies. You can tell them about any low-interest card offers you are receiving and ask them to match it to keep your business. Credit card companies are more likely to lower your rate if you have had the card for a long time and pay on time. If the customer service representative does not offer you a lower rate, ask to speak to a supervisor. If you still can't get a lower rate, call back later. Another customer service representative may agree to your terms. If you still don't get a rate reduction, keep making payments on time and wait a few months before asking again. Even if you transfer a balance to another card, you can try negotiating a lower interest rate on any other credit cards you have.

Consolidation

Debt consolidation is another way to reduce interest rates. Debt consolidation is taking out a new loan, at a lower interest rate, to pay

INTEREST RATES

Loan agreements explain how much interest the debtor pays for using the principal, or the amount of the loan. Sometimes a high interest rate is good—for example, if you have an interest-earning bank account, you want to earn as much interest as possible. If you are using a credit card, however, you should look for a low interest rate to pay as little as possible to the creditor.

Simple interest is a rate that does not increase over the term of the loan. If you borrow $100 at 10 percent interest for one year, you will pay the creditor $110.

Many types of loans, such as credit card loans, charge debtors compound interest. Compound interest is charged on the principal as well as on the accumulated interest. The interest compounds at set times, for example annually or quarterly (four times a year). With compound interest, the debtor is paying interest on interest.

If you are paying high interest rates, you can find ways to reduce them. If you are a good customer and pay credit card bills on time, you can ask for a reduced rate. You may also consider debt consolidation loans, balance transfers, personal loans (at a lower interest rate) to pay off debt, and debt-relief programs.

off other debts. In addition to a lower rate, consolidation can help the debtor by allowing lower monthly payments that are easier to make, and thus simplifying the payment process. For example, instead of making a credit card payment, mortgage payment, and car payment, you can make one payment to the new lender.

Other types of consolidation include home equity loans and lines of credit. The federal government offers consolidation for people with multiple student loans. Consolidation offers may be made by private companies and financial institutions including banks and credit unions. Secured loans require collateral, which is something the debtor owns that can be used to back the loan, such as a house or the title of a car. Secured loans usually have lower interest rates than unsecured debt consolidation loans and are often easier to qualify for. You may also qualify for a tax deduction for a secured loan, but if you fail to repay the loan you risk losing your collateral.

Debt-Relief Programs

Debt-relief programs may help you, but you may take a big hit at tax time. The government sees debt forgiveness as income, and you may have to pay taxes on the debt. If you don't pay taxes, you could be fined and charged interest, too. If that happens, you may end up with bigger financial problems. Carefully consider the consequences of debt-relief programs before going that route. You should also be sure you understand the terms of any agreements, such as fees the agency may charge you, and how the agency is earning money from helping you. This might be a percentage of your payments, for example.

Personal Loans

You may seek a personal loan to consolidate debts such as credit cards. A local bank or credit union might give you very favorable terms on such a loan if you qualify with an interest rate that is much lower than your original debts. You may be able to reduce the monthly payments as well. Analyze the long-term cost of a personal loan to make sure it is in your best interest. Be sure you understand the terms and what it will cost you.

Credit Counseling

A credit counselor can help you manage money and debt. You can find nonprofit credit counseling organizations along with private companies. You may be able to find one through your financial institution, workplace, credit union, or school. However, even nonprofit groups may charge fees, so be aware of the cost of such services before enrolling.

Also ask about counselors' certification and the type of training they have had. Credit counselors can help you create a budget and then stick to it.

HOW TO CHOOSE A REPUTABLE CREDIT COUNSELOR

The Federal Trade Commission offers advice on how to choose a reputable credit counselor. Here are some questions to ask to help you find the best counselor for you.

- **What services do you offer?** Look for an organization that offers a range of services, including budget counseling, and savings and debt management classes. Avoid organizations that push a debt management plan (DMP) as your only option before they spend a significant amount of time analyzing your financial situation.
- **Do you offer information?** Are educational materials available for free? Avoid organizations that charge for information.
- **In addition to helping me solve my immediate problem, will you help me develop a plan for avoiding problems in the future?**
- **What are your fees?** Are there set-up and/or monthly fees? Get a specific price quote in writing.
- **What if I can't afford to pay your fees or make contributions?** If an organization won't help you because you can't afford to pay, look elsewhere for help.
- **Will I have a formal written agreement or contract with you?** Don't sign anything without reading it first. Make sure all verbal promises are in writing.
- **Are you licensed to offer your services in my state?**
- **What are the qualifications of your counselors?** Are they accredited or certified by an outside organization? If so, by whom? If not, how are they trained? Try to use an organization whose counselors are trained by a non-affiliated party.
- **What assurance do I have that information about me (including my address, phone number, and financial information) will be kept confidential and secure?**
- **How are your employees paid?** Are they paid more if I sign up for certain services, if I pay a fee, or if I make a contribution to your organization? If the answer is yes, consider it a red flag and go elsewhere for help.

SOURCE: Federal Trade Commission
https://www.consumer.ftc.gov/articles/0153-choosing-credit-counselor

This budget should include an analysis of your spending and suggestions of how you can save money or earn more income. They can help you assess your individual financial situation and develop a plan to avoid debt problems in the future.

Debt Management Plans

If you are more than $3,000 in debt and are unable to repay what you owe, you may need to consider a debt management plan (DMP).

Before enrolling, research the organization or business. For example, visit the Better Business Bureau website bbb.org to look for complaints. The Federal Trade Commission offers advice on how to choose a credit counselor and evaluate a DMP at: https://www.consumer.ftc.gov/articles/0153-choosing-credit-counselor or you can choose from the FTC's list of approved credit counselors at the back of this volume.

You can also find a certified credit counselor through the National Foundation for Credit Counseling at: https://www.nfcc.org/our-services/credit-debt-counseling/debt-management-plan. A credit counseling organization can set up a DMP by developing a payment schedule with your creditors. The creditors may agree to certain terms, such as reduced interest rates or fees. You then deposit money with the credit counseling organization, which makes the payments. You should be able to set up automatic transfer of the funds with your bank.

The payment plan should be on a timetable so you know at the start how long it will take to pay off your debt—terms are usually three to five years. Discuss with the counselor the types of debt that can be included—it may include student loans and medical bills as well as credit card debt. Make sure that the monthly payment is something you can afford before enrolling in a DMP.

DMPs have some drawbacks, however. You may be required to cut up credit cards and agree to avoid making any charges while you are enrolled—if so, you should have a plan to deal with any emergency that comes up, such as a medical bill or job loss. If you do not have any savings, will the payment plan allow you to put any money aside for emergencies?

USE CAUTION WHEN SHOPPING FOR DEBT RELIEF SERVICES

Avoid any debt relief organization — whether it's credit counseling, debt settlement, or any other service — that:

- Charges any fees before it settles your debts or enters you into a DMP plan
- Pressures you to make "voluntary contributions," which is really another name for fees
- Touts a "new government program" to bail out personal credit card debt
- Guarantees it can make your unsecured debt go away
- Tells you to stop communicating with your creditors, but doesn't explain the serious consequences
- Tells you it can stop all debt collection calls and lawsuits
- Guarantees that your unsecured debts can be paid off for pennies on the dollar
- Won't send you free information about the services it provides without requiring you to provide personal financial information, like your credit card account numbers, and balances
- Tries to enroll you in a debt relief program without reviewing your financial situation with you
- Offers to enroll you in a DMP without teaching you budgeting and money management skills
- Demands that you make payments into a DMP before your creditors have accepted you into the program

Watch out for Debt Scams too!

Advance Fee Loans: Some companies guarantee you a loan if you pay them a fee in advance. The fee may range from $100 to several hundred dollars. Resist the temptation to follow up on these advance-fee loan guarantees. They may be illegal. It's true that many legitimate creditors offer extensions of credit through telemarketing and require an application or appraisal fee in advance. But legitimate creditors never guarantee that you will get the loan – or even represent that a loan is likely. Under the FTC's Telemarketing Sales Rule, a seller or telemarketer who guarantees or represents a high likelihood of your getting a loan or some other extension of credit, may not ask for — or accept — payment until you get the loan.

Credit Repair: Be suspicious of claims from so-called credit repair clinics. Many companies appeal to people with poor credit histories, promising to clean up their credit reports for a fee. But anything these companies can do for you for a fee, you can do yourself — for free. You have the right to correct inaccurate information in your file, but no one — regardless of their claims — can remove accurate negative information from your credit report. Only time and a conscientious effort to repay your debts will improve your credit report. Federal — and some state — laws ban these companies from charging you a fee until the services are fully performed.

SOURCE: Federal Trade Commission
https://www.consumer.ftc.gov/articles/0150-coping-debt

If the credit counseling organization fails to make a payment, you are responsible and it will affect your credit history, so check your monthly statements carefully and ensure any rate changes have been applied as well. Make sure the statements from the creditors and credit counseling agency agree.

Participation in a DMP will appear on your credit record. If you drop out, you will lose the repayment terms negotiated with your creditors, including interest rate reductions.

A DMP is one of three major types of debt consolidation. Others are debt consolidation loans and debt settlement.

Debt Settlement Companies

Debt settlement companies may negotiate a reduced debt with your creditors. This means you owe less and can get out of debt more quickly. However, the debt settlement company does not negotiate this deal at the start. Instead, you are expected to send the company a monthly check, which the company holds in an escrow account. During this time, your debt continues to grow as interest accrues and fees may be charged.

When the escrow account reaches a dollar goal, which may take a few months or years, the settlement company contacts your creditors and offers a lump sum payment. The creditors may or may not accept the offer. The debt settlement company charges you fees for the service, though you should not have to pay this until the debt has been settled. Be sure you understand the terms and read the contract carefully.

Using a debt settlement companies has some major drawbacks. Your participation remains on your credit report for seven years and can have a big effect on your credit score. The Internal Revenue Service (IRS) often classifies forgiven debt as income, so you may be burdened with a large income tax payment. Debt settlement programs may work for credit card debt and other unsecured debt through private lenders, but these programs are not accepted for some debt, such as student loans.

Student Loans

Student loans may be federal or private, and some have unique terms. If you have difficulty paying your student loans, you should contact the loan servicer and discuss your situation. Ask about changing your repayment plan or seeking temporary relief from making payments. However, such changes may incur interest and even fees for some loans. A great deal of information about student loans is available through the US Department of Education at: https://studentaid.ed.gov/sa/.

Consolidations

You may be able to consolidate several federal student loans with a direct consolidation loan. This allows you to pay off your student loans and instead make one monthly payment on the new loan. This process does not require you to pay a fee. Always carefully consider the terms of a consolidation. You may be able to negotiate lower monthly payments, though you may significantly extend the time you spend paying off the debt. This could mean you will pay more interest. Compare your current terms to any offer and be sure you understand the interest rate of the new, consolidated loan. You may also have enjoyed some borrower benefits with your original loans—such as

interest rate discounts, principal rebates, and loan cancellation benefits—that you will lose if you consolidate.

Deferment & Forbearance

If you are temporarily experiencing financial problems, you might instead consider a deferment or forbearance.

Deferment is a period when repayment of the loan principal and interest are temporarily delayed. You may not have to pay additional interest, depending on the loan. You can learn more about the terms and qualifications for various types of loans at: https://studentaid.ed.gov/sa/repay-loans/deferment-forbearance.

If you don't qualify for a deferment, you may be able to qualify for **forbearance**. This allows you to stop making payments, or reduces the size of payments, for up to a year. You will still be charged the interest on the debt. The lender may grant discretionary forbearance in cases of financial hardship or illness. You may receive mandatory forbearance in some situations, including participation in a medical or dental internship or residency program, if you are a member of the National Guard and have been activated by a governor, and if you are seeking teacher loan forgiveness by performing a qualifying teaching service.

TYPES OF STUDENT LOANS

FEDERAL STUDENT LOANS
William D. Ford Federal Direct Loan Program
- **Direct subsidized loans**, which are for students with financial need enrolled in undergraduate or career school programs.
- **Direct unsubsidized loans**, which are for students in undergraduate, graduate, and professional programs who do not demonstrate financial need.
- **Direct PLUS Loans**, which may cover educational expenses other loans do not. These loans are made to the student and parents and require a credit check for parents.
- **Direct Consolidation Loans**, which may enable students to combine federal student loans into one loan, eliminating the need to make multiple payments.

Federal Perkins Loan Program
Funds for Perkins loans come from the school and are available to students with dire financial need. As of February 2017, undergraduate students could borrow up to $5,500 per year through Perkins loans, while graduate students could borrow up to $8,000 annually. Not all schools participate in the Federal Perkins Loan Program, however.

STATE LOANS
You may also qualify for state loans, either in the state where you live or in the state where you go to school. Contact your school's financial aid office or visit your state's Department of Education website for more information.

PRIVATE LOANS
Private loans are similar to personal loans. The financial institution to which you apply will look at your credit history to decide if you are eligible for an education loan and to set the interest rate. The terms of federal student loans—including interest rates—are generally better than private education loans. You will probably benefit most if you turn to private sources only if federal loans will not cover your education costs. Some lenders may charge fees, which could offset any low interest rates and actually cost you more.

Consult Financial Literacy Basics: Tips for Paying Back Student Loans for more information.

Income-Based Repayment Plans

If you are not making enough money to repay your student loans, you may be eligible for an income-based repayment (IBR) plan. This means the amount you pay is based on the amount you earn. Contact your loan servicer to find out about this plan and visit the following for more information: https://studentaid.ed.gov/sa/repay-loans/understand/plans/income-driven.

Debt Forgiveness

Student loans may be forgiven through programs such as teacher loan forgiveness or public service loan forgiveness. Loans may also be forgiven due to disability,

Some student loans may be cancelled or forgiven in some circumstances. These include disability, death, bankruptcy, and programs such as teacher loan forgiveness or public service loan forgiveness. Federal Perkins Loans, for example, may be cancelled (in full or part) if you volunteer with the Peace Corps or ACTION programs, work as a nurse or medical technician, or work in Head Start, among other activities. If you are hoping to get public loan forgiveness, you should enroll in an IBR plan. You must make your monthly payments for 120 months before you qualify for loan forgiveness. For more information about loan forgiveness, see: https://studentaid.ed.gov/sa/repay-loans/forgiveness-cancellation. Discuss your situation with your loan provider.

Bankruptcy

You may have looked at all the numbers—your income, loans, and bills—and just can't figure out a way to pay your bills and get out of debt someday. If you can't find any way to pay off debt, either through budgeting or debt-reduction options, you may have to think about bankruptcy.

Bankruptcy is a legal status. Personal bankruptcy can clear your slate of most debt. It may stop wage garnishment (when the government has your employer withhold some of your pay) and foreclosure. Sounds good, right? But choosing this option has some severe drawbacks. It usually costs money, because you will probably need a bankruptcy lawyer. (The American Bar Association may be able to help if you are unable to afford a lawyer: http://www.americanbar.org/groups/legal_services/flh-home.html.)

Bankruptcy will remain on your credit report for seven to ten years. It will have a negative impact on your credit in the future. Experts say bankruptcy offers the most help to those with more than $15,000 in debt.

Bankruptcy cannot discharge some types of debt, including alimony, child support, debt incurred after filing for bankruptcy, some student loans, and some taxes. It also cannot discharge debt from personal injury to another person caused by the debtor (such as driving under the influence), and offers no protection to cosigners of your debts.

Some forms of bankruptcy are for businesses or municipalities and others are for individuals and couples. Chapter 7 bankruptcy is the most common chapter of personal bankruptcy. It remains on your credit report for ten years. Under this chapter, some of your property is sold and the proceeds are used to pay creditors. Chapter 13 bankruptcy remains on your credit report for seven years. It is the second-most-common chapter of bankruptcy under which people file. Chapter 13 allows individuals with regular incomes to have their debts adjusted and pay the debts over a period of time under this plan, usually three to five years.

Most debtors are required to undergo credit counseling before filing for bankruptcy. Some property, such as a primary home, may be exempt from sale to settle debts. The court may deny a debtor a discharge for several reasons, including if the debtor withholds information about finances, conceals or fraudulently transfers property, or commits perjury (lies under oath).

 **Ways to Save**

The more you save, the more you can use to pay off debt or avoid incurring additional debt.

Some big savings could come from selling a car and using public transportation, finding a less-expensive apartment or house, or getting a roommate (or several) to share living expenses if your lease allows. In some areas, you may be able to share a car or pay only when you need to use one. You may find a lower-cost insurance plan. In addition to these big decisions, you may be able to save money in other areas of your life as well.

If you use a debit card, you could be paying fees for many transactions. Find out if your financial institution limits your free monthly uses of the card. You may want to consider withdrawing the cash you will be using from each paycheck in one

transaction rather than in several. Maybe you can use only automatic teller machines (ATM) owned by your bank or credit union.

Compare utility rates and cell phone plans. You might find a lower rate by switching electricity providers, for example. Browse rates in your area on websites such as https://www.electricrate.com. Be sure to check the terms of the rate, which may be for several months or a year, and look for any fees involved.

You may also be able to get assistance with home energy costs through a program for low-income households. Visit www.benefits.gov for information and eligibility requirements. If you pay a monthly cell phone rate as part of a plan, consider how you use the phone. If you pay for unlimited data but don't use much each month, or use the phone only for emergencies, you may save money with a pay-as-you-go plan.

Are you spending too much money on food? You can save on grocery bills by shopping at discount stores, clipping coupons, finding sales, and buying in bulk. Use weekly sales circular to plan your meals for the week, and stick to your list—you will eliminate waste and avoid running out of food mid-week. Plan to use leftovers in another meal—grilled chicken can be dinner one day, and leftovers can be used on salad or in a casserole another day.

- Buy food that's on sale.
- Create a shopping list and stick to it.
- Plan your meals for the week, and use up leftovers.
- Compare unit prices to get the best deal.

Use store rewards cards to take advantage of special offers and sales. Scan the shelves for the unit price of items—this allows you to compare costs of different sizes of items. If the unit price per ounce of a large package is higher than the unit price for smaller packages, the large size is not the best price. Buy large packages of food to get the best deals. Meat can be expensive, so consider going meatless one or more days a week. Get your protein from less-expensive options, such as beans and lentils, eggs, cheese, seeds and nuts, and canned tuna.

Is your money disappearing into snack vending machines? Buy a large

package of treats and divide it into individual portions. Buy bags of veggies and carry servings to work for a healthy snack. Drink more water and less soda. A small bottle of water flavoring is a good buy if you don't like plain water, because it will flavor many glasses or bottles of water for a fraction of the cost of flavored drinks. Instead of stopping for daily coffees, buy a coffee maker and brew your own for much less—the money you save on coffee shops will quickly pay for the new appliance.

If you spend a lot of money on entertainment, such as restaurant meals and movies, consider cutting back on going out.

- Find less-expensive places, or go out for lunch instead of dinner— the prices are usually lower for the same meals.

- You might try getting together with like-minded friends who also want to cut back on spending. Instead of dining out, dine in— organize a potluck night or make a large amount of an inexpensive food, such as a casserole.

- Instead of going to an evening show, attend a movie matinee, when many theaters have a lower admission price. Some communities also have theaters that show second-run films, which may be less expensive.

- If you stream music, consider a less-costly streaming service.

- Can you reduce your cable television package or find a new cable provider? Does a streaming service offer shows or movies you like? Maybe you can eliminate the need for a subscription altogether—rent weekly movies or borrow them from a library.

Plan Ahead

While you are paying down your debt, try to put even a small amount aside. Once you have reduced debt, focus more attention on building up your savings.

Put aside some money each month to create an emergency fund that will cover all your living expenses for several months. Some experts suggest having six months of wages saved. This can protect you from getting into debt because of an unexpected illness, car repair, job loss, or some other problem in the future.

If your employer offers any matching funds toward a retirement plan, take advantage of it. Every dollar will help you reach retirement and stay out of debt when you are no longer working.

Credit Scores

Banks and credit card companies use credit scores to decide whether to extend credit to you or provide a loan. Anyone age eighteen or older can have a credit score, but many companies won't offer credit cards to anyone younger than twenty-one unless they have an authorized user, such as a parent, on the card account.

People and businesses talk about "good" credit scores, but it depends on what the score is for. To get a mortgage, loan, or credit cards, you will need a credit score that is good for that type of loan. About 90 percent of credit companies use scores calculated using Fair Isaac Corporation (FICO) software, though some use VantageScore, PLUS Score, TransRisk Score, or Equifax Score, which are similarly calculated. FICO scores are based on a person's ability to repay a loan, and are calculated based on information about you and many other people in similar situations. To have a FICO score, you usually need to have at least one account that has been open for at least six months. Your payment history—whether you pay your bills on time every time—is very important in calculating your score. According to FICO, 35 percent of your score is based on payment history. Another 30 percent is based on how much you owe (how much credit is available), 15 percent on the length of your credit history (longer history equals less risk), 10 percent on your new credit (if you've opened multiple new credit accounts), and 10 percent on the variety of credit you have (revolving credit lines, such as credit cards; installment debt such as car loans and student loans).

The credit bureaus—Equifax, Experian, and TransUnion—use FICO to calculate scores for people based on the information the credit bureaus have, so each may give the same person a different credit score. The bureaus look at how much you've borrowed, how much you owe, and your payment history. Companies usually offer their best terms, such as low interest rates, to people with the best credit scores. They want to loan money to people who are most likely to repay the loans. With a good credit score, you are more likely to have a loan approved. You may also have to agree to a credit check when you apply for a job, because potential employers may see you as more reliable and trustworthy if you have a good credit history. Some landlords also evaluate potential tenants using credit history, because they want to be sure you will pay your rent, and it can even affect your ability to get utilities hooked up because you may have to pay a deposit or find someone who will agree to pay your bills if you don't. Your credit score may affect your insurance rates in some states.

FICO scores range from 300 to 850— a higher score means a lower risk. In very general terms, a score of 650 or lower is usually seen as bad credit. FICO scores from 651 to 700 are considered fair, while scores from 701 to 759 are regarded as good. Any FICO score of 760 or higher is considered excellent credit.

For a mortgage, a minimum of 500 is usually needed for a Federal Housing Administration (FHA) loan, and at least 620 for other types of mortgages. People with a score of at least 760 are likely to get the lowest interest rate, which means they are likely to have lower monthly payments and pay less interest over the term of the mortgage. People with better credit scores are likely to qualify for larger loan amounts as well.

Experts say that the best credit card rewards offers go to those with credit scores of at least 720. The credit card companies offer very little information about how they make credit decisions, however. Carefully evaluate any offer.

Some experts believe a credit score of at least 720 should allow a borrower to get a low interest rate on a car loan. Sub-prime car loans may be available with much lower scores in the range of 500. As with mortgages, a better credit score should help you get a loan with better terms, so you could pay less each month and less interest overall.

CHECK YOUR CREDIT SCORE

You're entitled to one free copy of your credit report every 12 months from each of the three nationwide credit reporting companies.

Order online from annualcreditreport.com, the only authorized website for free credit reports, or call 1-877-322-8228. You will need to provide your name, address, social security number, and date of birth to verify your identity.

SOURCE: Federal Trade Commission
https://www.ftc.gov/faq/consumer-protection/get-my-free-credit-report

Building Good Credit

You can build good credit even if you don't have a credit history. First, establish a budget to understand how much you earn and how much you owe. A budget will help you make sure you pay your bills on time, which will help establish your credit history. Next you can focus on building good credit through credit cards and diversified credit, such as a small personal loan or student or auto loan.

You can probably qualify for a credit card for people who are building credit. These include student credit cards, although you will probably have to get a parent to co-sign your application. This means the co-signer is responsible for paying the bill if you don't. If you are able to save some money, you can get a secured credit card. For these cards, you deposit money to open the card. The issuer will use the deposit as collateral if you don't pay your bill. Secured credit cards are usually basic, meaning they don't offer users special features. Before applying, be sure the company reports to the credit bureaus so your account helps build your credit score. Many people build credit by getting a retail credit card from a store, such as a department store, where they shop. These cards usually have high interest rates and low credit limits.

You may want to diversify the types of loans you have with a small loan. You might take out a small personal loan

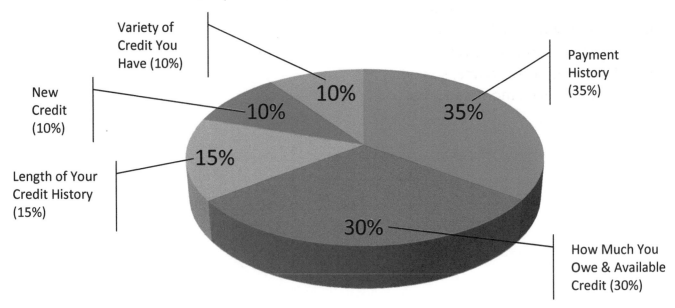

CREDIT SCORE CALCULATIONS

- Variety of Credit You Have (10%)
- New Credit (10%)
- Length of Your Credit History (15%)
- Payment History (35%)
- How Much You Owe & Available Credit (30%)

Pie chart values: 10%, 10%, 10%, 15%, 35%, 30%

and pay it back quickly. You may want to get a student loan if you need one, or a car loan. It's important to be sure you can afford to repay any loans, on time, to build good credit.

Maintaining Good Credit

You can maintain good credit by paying your bills on time. It's even better if you can make more than the minimum payment to repay the loan quickly. This will help you to pay less interest. As your credit score improves, your lenders may give you more credit. For example, your credit card limit might go up. Be sure you don't charge more than you can afford just because it's available. Your minimum monthly payments will also get larger, and this could make it more difficult for you to pay your bills on time. If you are having trouble making minimum monthly payments, contact your credit card companies and ask them to set up an alternative payment plan. They may agree to waive late charges or give you a lower monthly payment or reduced interest rate. You may also consider a balance transfer credit card to eliminate some payments and lower your interest rate.

A longer credit history helps your credit score. Even if you have credit

cards that you don't use, keeping them can boost your score. You can cut them up or keep them for an emergency. Any card with an annual fee is probably not worth keeping, however, because you can use that money elsewhere. Since 30 percent of your credit score is based on available credit, you can pay off some debt to improve your score. Credit card usage counts more in this area than other types of debt. Try to use no more than 10 percent of your available credit. This means that if your credit card limit is $1,000, you should charge no more than $100.

Credit checks can affect your credit score. Many credit inquiries can lower your score, so if you are applying for a loan, try to work quickly. File applications within about a thirty-day period if you can. Many credit checks within two weeks will usually only count as one inquiry for FICO.

Checking Your Credit Report

You are entitled, by law, every year to a free copy of your credit report from each of the three major credit bureaus. Visit AnnualCeditReport.com to request your reports. They don't include your credit scores, but you will see the information used to calculate your score. You can also contact FICO or another credit bureau to purchase reports with credit scores. Some sites that offer free credit score reports may offer only a score based on information rather than the FICO score. Some banks and credit card companies may also provide FICO scores to customers.

Experts recommend that you get copies of your credit report from all three major credit reporting agencies. The reports will include identifying information, credit history, public records, and inquiries. Check the identifying information for accuracy. Your name may be spelled multiple ways, for example, because several companies may have provided variations. The credit history section includes information about your creditors and accounts, including how much you owe, other names on the accounts, status of the loans, and your payment history. Some reports include the amount of each payment. Some may include notes, for example, "charged off," which means the creditor has given up on ever collecting the debt. The public records section includes any information such as bankruptcies, judgments, and tax liens. It does not include information about arrests, lawsuits, or any other information that is not related to finances. The inquiries section provides information about everyone who has requested your credit report, including

landlords, banks, and credit card companies. Hard inquiries are those you have set in motion, for example, when you apply for a credit card. Soft inquiries are from creditors who are monitoring your account, potential employers, and companies that want to prescreen you for offers of credit.

A government study in 2013 found that one in five consumers had errors on their credit reports from the three major bureaus. One in twenty errors cost the consumers financially, in the form of higher interest rates, for example. You can take steps to correct mistakes by disputing them with the credit bureau. Each report includes contact information for the credit bureau that provided it and an online dispute form. The credit bureaus will investigate by contacting the creditors, who have up to 45 days to respond. While the dispute is being investigated, the information you are challenging will show on the credit report as under dispute. If you are unsatisfied with the investigation, you can file a complaint online with the Consumer Financial Protection Bureau at: (https://www.consumerfinance.gov/complaint/#credit-reporting).

If you prefer to dispute a credit report by mail, circle the information that you are disputing on a copy of the report. Write a letter that explains what you are disputing and include your explanation. Request that the company remove or correct the information. The letter should include your complete name and address, the date, the complete name and address of the credit bureau, and a list of enclosures (a copy of the credit report, copies of bills showing payment, etc.). Your letter might say, for example:

Dear Sir or Madam:

I dispute the following information in my file, which I have circled and numbered on the enclosed copy of the credit report I received.

Item 1 [identify the name of source and type of item, such as credit account] is [inaccurate or incomplete] because [explain why it is inaccurate or incomplete]. I am requesting that [the item be removed, corrected, etc.] to correct this information.
[Item 2, etc., as needed.]

Enclosed are copies of [payment records, court documents, or any other proof you can provide] supporting my position. Please investigate this matter and [correct or delete] the items listed as soon as possible.

Sincerely,
[Your name]

Payday Loans

Payday loans are short-term loans that are due on your next payday. These are usually for small amounts (often up to $500). To get the loan you must give the lender access to your checking account or give the lender a check in advance for the full balance, which the lender is able to deposit when the loan comes due.

The terms of these loans vary with the lender. The loans may be due in one lump-sum payment, or paid in small installments over time. The lender may give the borrower cash, a check, or a prepaid debit card, or deposit the money electronically into your checking account. Both the amount you can borrow and the fees charged may be subject to state laws. The finance charge, or cost of the loan, varies: It could be $10 to $30 for every $100 borrowed. These high finance charges are equal to high annual percentage rates (APR) of

possibly several hundred percent (credit card APRs range from 12 percent to 30 percent).

Predatory Lending Practices

Some payday loans are considered predatory lending practices, because the borrower can't afford to pay them. Predatory lending is any practice that inflicts abusive or unfair loan terms on a borrower, or uses coercive, deceptive, exploitative, or unscrupulous actions to persuade a borrower to accept the terms for a loan the borrower can't afford or doesn't need or want. Many include high fees and costs, such as document preparation charges, that are not clearly explained or found buried in the fine print.

Predatory lenders often target people who are poor, uneducated, or desperate—for example, someone who has no way to pay the bill for a car or home repair or a medical emergency. Many people with poor credit who cannot qualify for lines of credit with a bank or other traditional sources fall victim to predatory lending practices.

Many people have lost their homes when they were unable to pay mortgages secured through predatory lending practices. For example, balloon mortgages refinance mortgages so the borrower has lower payments at first. Later, however, the payments grow larger and larger, until the borrower can no longer make them. The lender then may offer another refinance, with high fees and interest. This is an example of how people can be trapped in a debt cycle.

Car title loans are common risky short-term loans. A borrower gets a small loan for a short time, pays a fee to the lender, and gives the lender the title to a vehicle. If the borrower is unable to repay the loan, the lender can take possession of the vehicle.

Always be cautious when considering any loan. Short-term loans can be particularly expensive. Instead, if you are faced with an unexpected debt, consider applying for a small loan from a credit union or other traditional financial institution or use a credit card. The terms of traditional loans are usually better, with lower interest rates. You may also be able to borrow money from family and friends. Repay the debt as quickly as possible, and focus on building up some savings for future emergencies.

Appendices

List of Approved Credit Counseling Agencies by the U.S. Department of Justice

#1$t Choice Credit Counseling Financial Education a/k/a DBS
2049 Marco Drive
Camarillo, CA 93010
877-692-5669
www.mybknow.com
Provides Services via: Internet
Additional Languages: Spanish
Operates in: AK, AZ, AR, CA, CO, CT, DE, DC, FL, GA, HI, ID, IL, IN, IA, KS, KY, LA, ME, MD, MA, MI, MN, MS, MO, MT, NE, NV, NH, NJ, NM, NY, ND, OH, OK, PA, PR, RI, SC, SD, TN, TX, UT, VT, VA, WA, WV, WI, WY

$$$$$Simple Class, Inc.
7007 Positano Hill Avenue
Las Vegas, NV 89178
866-742-6259
www.simpleclass.net
Provides Services via: Internet
Operates in: AK, AZ, AR, CA, CO, CT, DE, DC, FL, GA, GU, HI, ID, IN, IA, KS, KY, LA, ME, MD, MI, MN, MS, MO, MT, NE, NV, NH, NJ, NM, NY, ND, MP, OH, OK, PA, PR, RI, SC, SD, TN, TX, UT, VT, VA, VI, WA, WV, WI, WY

1$ Wiser Consumer Education, Inc.
503 Hillcrest Lane
Krum, TX 76249
800-496-2440
www.1dollarwiser.com
Provides Services via: Internet, Telephone
Operates in: AK, AZ, AR, CA, CO, CT, DE, DC, FL, GA, GU, HI, ID, IL, IN, IA, KS, KY, LA, ME, MD, MA, MI, MN, MS, MO, MT, NE, NV, NH, NJ, NM, NY, ND, MP, OH, OK, OR, PA, PR, RI, SC, SD, TN, TX, UT, VT, VA, VI, WA, WV, WI, WY

123 Credit Counselors, Inc
6161 Blue Lagoon Drive
Suite 255A
Miami, FL 33126
888-412-2123
www.a123cc.org
Provides Services via: Internet, Telephone, In Person
Additional Languages: Spanish
Operates in: AK, AZ, AR, CA, CO, CT, DE, DC, FL, GA, GU, HI, ID, IL, IN, IA, KS, KY, LA, ME, MD, MA, MI, MN, MS, MO, MT, NE, NV, NH, NJ, NM, NY, ND, MP, OH, OK, OR, PA, PR, RI, SC, SD, TN, TX, UT, VT, VA, VI, WA, WV, WI, WY

Abacus Credit Counseling

17337 Ventura Boulevard
Suite 226
Encino, CA 91316

800-516-3834
www.abacuscc.org

Provides Services via: Internet, Telephone
Additional Languages: Spanish
Operates in: AK, AZ, AR, CA, CO, CT, DE, DC, FL, GA, GU, HI, ID, IL, IN, IA, KS, KY, LA, ME, MD, MA, MI, MN, MS, MO, MT, NE, NV, NH, NJ, NM, NY, ND, MP, OH, OK, OR, PA, PR, RI, SC, SD, TN, TX, UT, VT, VA, VI, WA, WV, WI, WY

Academy of Financial Literacy, Inc.

725 W. Elliot Road
Gilbert, AZ 85233

877-833-2867
www.academyoffinancialliteracy.com

Provides Services via: Internet
Additional Languages: Spanish
Operates in: AK, AZ, AR, CA, CO, CT, DE, DC, FL, GA, GU, HI, ID, IL, IN, IA, KS, KY, LA, ME, MD, MA, MI, MN, MS, MO, MT, NE, NV, NH, NJ, NM, NY, ND, MP, OH, OK, PA, PR, RI, SC, SD, TN, TX, UT, VT, VA, VI, WA, WV, WI, WY

Advantage Credit Counseling Service, Inc.

River Park Commons
2403 Sidney Street, Suite 400
Pittsburgh, PA 15203

888-511-2227
www.advantageccs.org

Provides Services via: Internet, Telephone, In Person
Operates in: AK, AZ, AR, CA, CO, CT, DE, DC, FL, GA, GU, HI, ID, IL, IN, IA, KS, KY, LA, ME, MD, MA, MI, MN, MS, MO, MT, NE, NV, NH, NJ, NM, NY, ND, OH, OK, OR, PA, PR, RI, SC, SD, TN, TX, UT, VT, VA, VI, WA, WV, WI, WY

Alliance Credit Counseling, Inc.

15720 Brixham Hill Avenue
Suite 575
Charlotte, NC 28277-4424

704-540-2477
www.knowdebt.org

Provides Services via: Internet, Telephone,
Additional Languages: Spanish
Operates in: AK, AZ, AR, CA, CO, CT, DE, DC, FL, GA, GU, HI, ID, IL, IN, IA, KS, KY, LA, ME, MD, MA, MI, MN, MS, MO, MT, NE, NV, NH, NJ, NM, NY, ND, MP, OH, OK, OR, PA, PR, RI, SC, SD, TN, TX, UT, VT, VA, VI, WA, WV, WI, WY

American Debt Resources, Inc.

384 Larkfield Road
East Northport, NY 11731

800-498-0766

www.americandebtresources.com

Provides Services via: Telephone, In Person
Additional Languages: Spanish
Operates in: AK, AZ, AR, CA, CO, CT, DE, DC, FL, GA, GU, HI, ID, IL, IN, IA, KS, KY, LA, ME, MD, MA, MI, MN, MS, MO, MT, NE, NV, NH, NJ, NM, NY, ND, MP, OH, OK, OR, PA, PR, RI, SC, SD, TN, TX, UT, VT, VA, VI, WA, WV, WI, WY

Aurora Family Service, Inc.

3200 W Highland Blvd.
Milwaukee, WI 53208

414-482-8801

www.creditcounselingwi.org

Provides Services via: Telephone, In Person
Additional Languages: Spanish
Operates in: WI

Black Hills Children's Ranch, Inc.

1644 Concourse Drive
Rapid City, SD 57703

605-348-1608

www.pioneercredit.com

Provides Services via: Internet, Telephone, In Person
Additional Languages: Spanish
Operates in: AK, AZ, AR, CA, CO, CT, DE, DC, FL, GA, GU, HI, ID, IL, IN, IA, KS, KY, LA, ME, MD, MA, MI, MN, MS, MO, MT, NE, NV, NH, NJ, NM, NY, ND, MP, OH, OK, OR, PA, PR, RI, SC, SD, TN, TX, UT, VT, VA, VI, WA, WV, WI, WY

Catholic Charities of the Diocese of Green Bay, Inc.

1825 Riverside Drive
Green Bay, WI 54301

920-272-8234

www.newcatholiccharities.org

Provides Services via: In Person
Additional Languages: Hmong, Spanish
Operates in: MI, WI

Catholic Charities of the Diocese of St. Cloud

157 Roosevelt Rd.
Suite 200
St. Cloud, MN 56301

320-650-1664

www.stcloud.org

Provides Services via: Telephone, In Person
Additional Languages: Spanish
Operates in: MN

Center for Child and Family Services, Inc.
2021 Cunningham Drive, Suite 400
Hampton, VA 23666
757-826-2227
www.debtfreeonline.com
Provides Services via: Internet, In Person
Operates in: VA

Chestnut Health Systems, Inc.
1003 Martin Luther King Drive
Bloomington, IL 61701
309-820-3501
www.chestnut.org/credit
Provides Services via: Internet, Telephone, In Person
Operates in: IL

Comprehensive Credit Counseling of Rural Services of Indiana
60918 US 31 South
South Bend, IN 46614
574-299-9648
www.comprehensivecreditcounseling.com
Provides Services via: Telephone, In Person
Operates in: IL, IN, IA, KS, KY, MI, MN, MO, OH, TN, WI

Consumer Credit Counseling Service of Buffalo, Inc.
40 Gardenville Parkway
Suite 300
West Seneca, NY 14224
716-712-2060
www.consumercreditbuffalo.org
Provides Services via: Internet, Telephone, In Person
Additional Languages: Spanish, Arabic, Armenian, Bosnian/Croatian/Serbian, Chinese
Operates in: AK, AZ, AR, CA, CO, CT, DE, DC, FL, GA, GU, HI, ID, IL, IN, IA, KS, KY,
LA, ME, MD, MA, MI, MN, MS, MO, MT, NE, NV, NH, NJ, NM, NY, ND, MP, OH,
OK, OR, PA, PR, RI, SC, SD, TN, TX, UT, VT, VA, VI, WA, WV, WI, WY

Consumer Credit Counseling Service of Delaware Valley dba Cl
1608 Walnut Street
10th Floor
Philadelphia, PA 19103
215-563-5665
www.clarifi.org
Provides Services via: Telephone, In Person
Additional Languages: Chinese,, Yue/Cantonese, Spanish, Chinese
Operates in: DE, NJ, PA

Consumer Credit Counseling Service of Huntington

1102 Memorial Blvd
Huntington, WV 25701

304-522-4321

www.goodwillhunting.org

Provides Services via: Telephone, In Person
Operates in: KY, OH, WV

Consumer Credit Counseling Service of Northeastern Iowa, Inc

1003 West 4th Street
Waterloo, IA 50702

319-234-0661

www.cccsia.org

Provides Services via: Internet, Telephone, In Person
Additional Languages: Spanish
Operates in: IL, IA, MN, NE, SD, WI

Consumer Credit Counseling Service of Northwest Indiana, Inc

800 E 86th Ave.
Suite B
Merrillville, IN 46410

219-980-4800

www.cccsnwi.org

Provides Services via: In Person
Operates in: IN

Consumer Credit Counseling Service of Puerto Rico, Inc.

1607 Avenue Ponce de Leon
EDIF Cobian's Plaza, Suite GM-9
San Juan, PR 00909

787-722-8835

www.consumerpr.org

Provides Services via: Internet, Telephone, In Person
Additional Languages: Spanish
Operates in: FL, PR, VI

Consumer Credit Counseling Service of San Francisco

1655 Grant Street
Suite 1300
Concord, CA 94520

800-777-7526

www.balancepro.org

Provides Services via: Internet, Telephone, In Person
Additional Languages: Spanish
Operates in: AK, AZ, AR, CA, CO, CT, DE, DC, FL, GA, HI, ID, IL, IN, IA, KS, KY, LA,
ME, MD, MA, MN, MS, MO, MT, NE, NV, NH, NJ, NM, NY, ND, OH, OK, OR, PA,
RI, SC, SD, TN, TX, UT, VT, VA, WA, WV, WI, WY

Consumer Credit Counseling Service of Southern Oregon, Inc.

820 Crater Lake Avenue
Suite 202
Medford, OR 97504

541-779-2273

www.cccsso.org

Provides Services via: Internet, In Person
Operates in: CA, OR

Consumer Credit Counseling Service of the Midwest, Inc.

4500 East Broad Street
Columbus, OH 43213

800-355-2227

www.apprisen.com

Provides Services via: Internet, Telephone, In Person
Additional Languages: Spanish, Swedish
Operates in: AK, AZ, AR, CA, CO, CT, DE, DC, FL, GA, HI, ID, IL, IN, IA, KS, KY, LA,
   ME, MD, MA, MI, MN, MS, MO, MT, NE, NV, NH, NJ, NM, NY, ND, OH, OK, OR,
   PA, PR, RI, SC, SD, TN, TX, UT, VT, VA, WA, WV, WI, WY

Consumer Credit Counseling Service, Inc.

1201 W. Walnut
Salina, KS 67401

785-827-6731

www.ksccs.org

Provides Services via: Internet, Telephone, In Person
Additional Languages: Spanish
Operates in: KS

Consumer Credit of Des Moines

6129 SW 63rd Street
Des Moines, IA 50321

515-287-6428

www.consumercredit-dm.com

Provides Services via: Internet, Telephone, In Person
Operates in: AK, AR, CA, FL, GA, HI, IL, IA, LA, MN, MS, MO, NE, NM, ND, OH, OK,
   OR, SC, SD, TN, TX, WA, WV

Consumer Debt Counselors, Inc.

831 W. Morse Blvd
Winter Park, FL 32789

800-820-9232

www.consumerdebtcounselors.com

Provides Services via: Internet, Telephone, In Person
Operates in: FL, GA, IL, LA, NY, WA

Consumer Education Services, Inc., DBA Start Fresh Today/DBA

3700 Barrett Drive
Raleigh, NC 27609

919-785-0725

www.startfreshtoday.com

Provides Services via: Internet, Telephone
Additional Languages: Spanish
Operates in: AK, AZ, AR, CA, CO, CT, DE, DC, FL, GA, GU, HI, ID, IL, IN, IA, KS, KY, LA, ME, MD, MA, MI, MN, MS, MO, MT, NE, NV, NH, NJ, NM, NY, ND, MP, OH, OK, OR, PA, PR, RI, SC, SD, TN, TX, UT, VT, VA, VI, WA, WV, WI, WY

Credit Card Management Services, Inc. d/b/a Debthelper.com

1325 N. Congress Ave.
Suite 201
West Palm Beach, FL 33401

800-920-2262

www.debthelper.com

Provides Services via: Internet, Telephone, In Person
Additional Languages: Spanish, French, Haitian, Creole, Portuguese, Gujarathi
Operates in: AK, AZ, AR, CA, CO, CT, DE, DC, FL, GA, GU, HI, ID, IL, IN, IA, KS, KY, LA, ME, MD, MA, MI, MN, MS, MO, MT, NE, NV, NH, NJ, NM, NY, ND, MP, OH, OK, OR, PA, PR, RI, SC, SD, TN, TX, UT, VT, VA, VI, WA, WV, WI, WY

Credit Counseling of Arkansas, Inc.

1111 Zion Road
Fayetteville, AR 72703

479-521-8877

www.ccoacares.com

Provides Services via: Telephone, In Person
Additional Languages: Marshallese, Spanish
Operates in: AR, MO, OK

Debt Counseling Corp.

3033 Express Drive North
Suite 103
Hauppauge, NY 11749

888-354-6332

www.debtcounselingcorp.org

Provides Services via: Internet, Telephone, In Person
Additional Languages: Spanish
Operates in: AK, AZ, AR, CA, CT, DC, FL, GA, HI, ID, IL, KS, KY, LA, ME, MD, MA, MI, MS, MO, NJ, NM, NY, ND, OH, OR, PA, SD, TN, TX, VA, WA, WV, WI, WY

Debt Management Credit Counseling Corp.

3310 N. Federal Highway
Lighthouse Point, FL 33064

954-418-1466
www.dmcccorp.org

Provides Services via: Telephone, In Person
Additional Languages: Spanish
Operates in: AK, AZ, AR, CA, CO, CT, DE, DC, FL, GA, HI, ID, IL, IN, IA, KS, KY, LA, ME, MD, MA, MI, MN, MS, MO, MT, NE, NV, NH, NJ, NM, NY, ND, OH, OK, OR, PA, PR, RI, SC, SD, TN, TX, UT, VT, VA, WA, WV, WI, WY

Debtor Ed's Credit Counseling Inc.

8956 Tuscan Valley Place
Orlando, FL 32825

844-529-9601
www.mydebtored.com

Provides Services via: Internet
Additional Languages: Spanish
Operates in: AK, AZ, AR, CA, CO, CT, DE, DC, FL, GA, GU, HI, ID, IL, IN, IA, KS, KY, LA, ME, MD, MA, MI, MN, MS, MO, MT, NE, NV, NH, NJ, NM, NY, ND, MP, OH, OK, OR, PA, PR, RI, SC, SD, TN, TX, UT, VT, VA, VI, WA, WV, WI, WY

Evergreen Financial Counseling

9747 Stonecrest Drive S.
Salem, OR 97306

800-581-3513
www.evergreenclass.com

Provides Services via: Internet, Telephone
Operates in: AK, AZ, AR, CA, CO, CT, DE, DC, FL, GA, GU, HI, ID, IL, IN, IA, KS, KY, LA, ME, MD, MA, MI, MN, MS, MO, MT, NE, NV, NH, NJ, NM, NY, ND, MP, OH, OK, OR, PA, PR, RI, SC, SD, TN, TX, UT, VT, VA, VI, WA, WV, WI, WY

Family Counseling Service of Northern Nevada, Inc.

575 E. Plumb Lane, Suite 101
Reno, NV 89502

775-322-6557
fcsnv.org

Provides Services via: Telephone, In Person
Additional Languages: Spanish
Operates in: NV

Family Foundations of Northeast Florida, Inc.

40 East Adams Street
Suite 320
Jacksonville, FL 32202

904-396-4846
www.familyfoundations.org

Provides Services via: Internet, Telephone, In Person
Operates in: FL

Family Service Agency, Inc.
628 West Broadway
Suite 102
North Little Rock, AR 72114
501-753-0202
www.helpingfamilies.org
Provides Services via: Internet
Operates in: AR, MS, OK, TN

Family Services of Southern Wisconsin and Northern Illinois,
416 College Street
Beloit, WI 53511
608-365-1244
www.cccsbeloit.org
Provides Services via: Internet, Telephone, In Person
Operates in: IL, WI

Financial Information Service Center, Inc.
1800 Appleton Road
Menasha, WI 54952
920-886-1000
www.fisc-cccs.org
Provides Services via: Internet, Telephone, In Person
Operates in: WI

Graceworks Lutheran Services
660 South Main Street
Suite 1S061
Dayton, OH 45402
937-643-2227
www.graceworksdebtcounseling.org
Provides Services via: Internet, Telephone, In Person
Operates in: OH

Hananwill Credit Counseling
115 North Cross Street
Robinson, IL 62454
877-544-5560
www.hananwill.com
Provides Services via: Internet, Telephone
Operates in: AZ, AR, CO, FL, GA, ID, IL, IN, IA, KS, KY, LA, MD, MA, MI, MN, MO, MT, NE, NV, NJ, OH, OK, PA, SD, TN, TX, VA, WA, WI

Housing and Credit Counseling, Inc.
1195 SW Buchanan
Suite 101
Topeka, KS 66604
785-234-0217
www.hcci-ks.org
Provides Services via: Telephone, In Person
Operates in: KS, MO

Institute for Consumer Credit Education

16335 South Harlem Avenue
Suite 400
Tinley Park, IL 60477

708-633-6355
www.icceillinois.org

Provides Services via: Telephone, In Person
Operates in: IL

iPayDebt Financial Services, Inc. d/b/a Cornerstone Financia

2806 Flintrock Trace #A101
Lakeway, TX 78738

800-336-1245
www.csfedu.org

Provides Services via: Internet, In Person
Additional Languages: Spanish
Operates in: AZ, CA, CO, CT, GA, ID, IL, IN, IA, KS, KY, ME, MD, MA, MI, MN, MS,
MO, MT, NE, NV, NH, NY, ND, OR, PA, SC, TN, TX, UT, VT, VA

Lutheran Social Services of South Dakota

705 East 41st Street
Suite 100
Sioux Falls, SD 57105

605-330-2700
www.lsssd.org

Provides Services via: Internet, Telephone, In Person
Additional Languages: Spanish
Operates in: IA, MN, NE, SD

Money Management International, Inc.

14141 Southwest Freeway
Suite 1000
Sugar Land, TX 77478-3494

(877) 964-2227
www.moneymanagement.org

Provides Services via: Internet, Telephone, In Person
Additional Languages: Spanish, Armenian, French, Laotian, Other,, Europe
Operates in: AK, AZ, AR, CA, CO, CT, DE, DC, FL, GA, GU, HI, ID, IL, IN, IA, KS, KY,
LA, ME, MD, MA, MI, MN, MS, MO, MT, NE, NV, NH, NJ, NM, NY, ND, MP, OH,
OK, OR, PA, PR, RI, SC, SD, TN, TX, UT, VT, VA, VI, WA, WV, WI, WY

National Debt Management, Inc.

17520 West 12 Mile Road
Suite 105
Southfield, MI 48076

248-200-2106
www.nationaldebtmgt.com

Provides Services via: Telephone, In Person
Additional Languages: Arabic
Operates in: CT, DE, GA, ME, MD, MA, MI, NH, NJ, NY, OH, PA, RI, SC, VT, VA, WV

Northwest Michigan Community Action Agency, Inc.

3963 Three Mile Road
Traverse City, MI 49686

231-947-3780
www.nmcaa.net

Provides Services via: In Person
Operates in: MI

Rushmore Consumer Credit Resource Center

2310 N. Maple Avenue
Rapid City, SD 57701

605-348-4550
www.cccsbh.com

Provides Services via: Internet
Operates in: NE, ND, SD, WY

Springboard Nonprofit Consumer Credit Management, Inc., dba

4351 Latham Street
Riverside, CA 92501

951-781-0114
www.bkhelp.org

Provides Services via: Internet, Telephone, In Person
Additional Languages: Spanish
Operates in: AK, AZ, AR, CA, CO, CT, DE, DC, FL, GA, GU, HI, ID, IL, IN, IA, KS, KY, LA, ME, MD, MA, MI, MN, MS, MO, MT, NE, NV, NH, NJ, NM, NY, ND, MP, OH, OK, OR, PA, PR, RI, SC, SD, TN, TX, UT, VT, VA, VI, WA, WV, WI, WY

Summit Financial Education, Inc.

4800 E. Flower Street
Tucson, AZ 85712

800-780-5965
www.summitfe.org

Provides Services via: Internet
Operates in: AK, AZ, AR, CA, CO, CT, DE, DC, FL, GA, HI, ID, IL, IN, IA, KS, KY, LA, ME, MD, MA, MI, MN, MS, MO, MT, NE, NV, NH, NJ, NM, NY, ND, OH, OK, OR, PA, PR, RI, SC, SD, TN, TX, UT, VT, VA, WA, WV, WI, WY

The Family Center of Columbus, Inc.

1350 15th Avenue
Columbus, GA 31901

706-327-3239
www.cccs-wga.com

Provides Services via: Internet, Telephone, In Person
Operates in: GA

The Mesquite Group, Inc.
463 W. Harwood Road
Hurst, TX 76054
817-769-4069
www.themesquitegroup.org
Provides Services via: Internet, Telephone
Additional Languages: Spanish
Operates in: AK, AZ, AR, CA, CO, CT, DE, DC, FL, GA, GU, HI, ID, IL, IN, IA, KS, KY, LA, ME, MD, MA, MI, MN, MS, MO, MT, NE, NV, NH, NJ, NM, NY, ND, MP, OH, OK, PA, PR, RI, SC, SD, TN, TX, UT, VT, VA, VI, WA, WV, WI, WY

Transformance, Inc.
8737 King George Drive
Suite 200
Dallas, TX 75235-2273
214-638-2227
www.transformanceusa.org
Provides Services via: Internet, Telephone, In Person
Additional Languages: Spanish
Operates in: AK, CA, CO, CT, DE, DC, FL, GA, HI, ID, IL, IN, IA, KS, KY, LA, ME, MD, MA, MI, MN, MS, MO, MT, NE, NH, NM, NY, ND, OH, OK, OR, PA, RI, SD, TN, TX, UT, VT, VA, WA, WV, WI, WY

Urgent Credit Counseling, Inc.
219 SW Stark Street
Suite 200
Portland, OR 97204
866-233-1940
www.urgentco.com
Provides Services via: Internet, Telephone
Additional Languages: Spanish
Operates in: AK, AZ, AR, CA, CO, CT, DE, DC, FL, GA, GU, HI, ID, IL, IN, IA, KS, KY, LA, ME, MD, MA, MI, MN, MS, MO, MT, NE, NV, NH, NJ, NM, NY, ND, MP, OH, OK, OR, PA, PR, RI, SC, SD, TN, TX, UT, VT, VA, VI, WA, WV, WI, WY

Where to Get a Free Credit Report

You're entitled to one free copy of your credit report every 12 months from each of the three nationwide credit reporting companies. Order online from **www.annualcreditreport.com**, the only authorized website for free credit reports, or call 1-877-322-8228. You will need to provide your name, address, social security number, and date of birth to verify your identity.

Beware of other "Free Credit Report" websites

Other websites that claim to offer "free credit reports," "free credit scores," or "free credit monitoring" are not part of the legally mandated free annual credit report program. In some cases, the "free" product comes with strings attached. For example, some sites sign you up for a supposedly "free" service that converts to one you have to pay for after a trial period. If you don't cancel during the trial period, you may be unwittingly agreeing to let the company start charging fees to your credit card.

Glossary

This glossary contains the most important terms used in this publication.

Bad Debt	Debt, such as credit card debt, that will not increase in value or help you earn more money.
Balance Transfer	Using a lower-interest or no-interest credit card to pay off a high-interest credit card.
Collateral	Something of value used to back up debt.
Compound Interest	Interest that must be paid on the principal amount and other interest added onto it.
Credit	Money that is given to you to use.
Debt	Money that is owed.
Debt-to-Income (DTI) Ratio	A comparison of your monthly income and debt; the lower the percentage, the better the ratio.
Debtor	A person who borrows money and owes a debt.
Deferment	A temporary delay on student loan payments without having to pay interest.
Fixed Expenses	Expenses, such as a mortgage payment, that do not vary from month to month.
Forbearance	Permission to stop making student loan payments or to make reduced student loan payments for up to a year while still paying interest.
Good Debt	Debt, such as student loans and a mortgage, that will help you earn more or increase in value.
Home-Equity Loan	A loan based on the value of your house.
Interest	Money a debtor must pay to borrow principal.
Principal	Amount of money borrowed, not including interest.
Secured Deb	Debt backed by something of value, such as a home.

Simple Interest   Interest based only on the principal.

Variable Expenses   Expenses, such as groceries, that vary from month
                                    to month.

SOURCES

https://www.debt.org/bankruptcy/

http://www.uscourts.gov/services-forms/bankruptcy/bankruptcy-basics/chapter-7-bankruptcy-basics

https://www.consumer.ftc.gov/articles/0153-choosing-credit-counselor

https://www.debt.org/consolidation/

https://www.debt.org/settlement/

https://studentaid.ed.gov/sa/repay-loans/consolidation

http://www.realsimple.com/work-life/money/eliminate-credit-card-debt

http://www.investopedia.com/articles/investing/020614/learn-simple-and-compound-interest.asp

https://www.discover.com/credit-cards/resources/balance-transfer

http://money.howstuffworks.com/personal-finance/debt-management/debt2.htm

http://www.bankrate.com/finance/credit-cards/want-a-lower-credit-card-rate-just-ask.aspx

https://www.debt.org/management-plans/

http://money.howstuffworks.com/personal-finance/debt-management/debt1.htm

https://www.wellsfargo.com/goals-credit/smarter-credit/credit-101/debt-to-income-ratio/

https://www.credit.org/2011/04/07/debt-to-income-ratio/

http://www.investopedia.com/terms/d/debt.asp

http://www.investopedia.com/terms/d/debtconsolidation.asp

http://www.businessinsider.com/compound-interest-and-credit-card-debt-2013-2

http://www.investopedia.com/articles/investing/020614/learn-simple-and-compound-interest.asp

https://www.thebalance.com/what-is-interest-315436

http://www.investopedia.com/ask/answers/042315/what-difference-between-compounding-interest-and-simple-interest.asp

http://www.investopedia.com/articles/investing/020614/learn-simple-and-compound-interest.asp

https://www.ftc.gov/faq/consumer-protection/get-my-free-credit-report

https://www.justice.gov/ust/list-credit-counseling-agencies-approved-pursuant-11-usc-111

https://www.consumer.ftc.gov/articles/0150-coping-debt

https://www.consumer.ftc.gov/articles/0155-free-credit-reports

https://greyhouse.weissratings.com

Financial Ratings Series, published by Weiss Ratings and Grey House Publishing offers libraries, schools, universities and the business community a wide range of investing, banking, insurance and financial literacy tools. Visit www.greyhouse.com or https://greyhouse.weissratings.com for more information about the titles and online tools below.

- Weiss Ratings Guide to Banks
- Weiss Ratings Guide to Credit Unions
- Weiss Ratings Guide to Health Insurers
- Weiss Ratings Guide to Property & Casualty Insurers
- Weiss Ratings Guide to Life & Annuity Insurers
- Weiss Ratings Investment Research Guide to Stocks
- Weiss Ratings Investment Research Guide to Bond & Money Market Mutual Funds
- Weiss Ratings Investment Research Guide to Stock Mutual Funds
- Weiss Ratings Investment Research Guide to Exchange-Traded Funds
- Weiss Ratings Consumer Guides
- Weiss Ratings Medicare Supplement Insurance Buyers Guide
- Financial Ratings Series Online – **https://greyhouse.weissratings.com**